Big Impact
A Rising Legacy

By
David K. Ewen, M.Ed.

Ambassador to the Nations
Civilian Sector
Business, Education, Technology

ISBN: 9781654240196

Imprint: Independently published

by Ewen Prime Company

I0792131

Contents

Preview
Author
Source
Scripture
Presentation

<u>PREVIEW</u>

Big Impact takes you on a behind-the-scenes journey of a United States Ambassador in the civilian sector showing sacrifices and diligence made to represent specialized core values and American ingenuity to the nations in the areas of business, education, and technology. It's a journey that leaves the impact of a legacy. It's a big impact from a rising legacy.

<u>AUTHOR</u>

Amb. David K. Ewen, M.Ed. speaks to the nations and is currently serving as a United States Ambassador in the civilian sector. He represents American ingenuity and concepts in the areas of business, education, and technology. David's office runs the *T.O.C.A. Enterprise 2061* staffed by a 45-member crowdsourced scalable on-demand workforce. Ambassador Ewen speaks to the nations reaching Asia, the Middle East, Europe, Russia, and South America. In 2020, he accepted his 2nd five-year term as Ambassador. David is an entrepreneur and business owner since 1994.   In America, he toured the 7 states of

New York and New England lecturing on 18 topics associated with global communication and entrepreneurial studies. His foundation of his lectures, in part, related to digital multimedia   technology. Ambassador Ewen is the author of several books and audiobooks. He has produced short films and TV shows that stream online.

<u>SOURCE</u>

The following is transcribed from audio from a radio show. The style of writing that you are about to read is conversational as if spoken.

<u>SCRIPTURE</u>

Jeremiah 29:11 (NIV) - For I know the plans I have for you," declares the Lord, "plans to prosper you and not to harm you, plans to give you hope and a future.

<u>PRESENTATION</u>

Hello. My name is David and I'm here to talk to you about what it's like to be an ambassador to the nations. My conversation today is not to have a parade or blow a horn that is self-serving. I do not speak to you in a prideful way. I am not presenting this to pat myself on my back. I'm sharing with you a journey that I have. It is not a common journey. It is a journey of sacrifice with significant rewards. My office has the burden of responsibility to show America in a positive light that effect future economic outcomes and international relationships.

My work is not done alone. I have and work closely with a team of 45 crowd-sourced positions. We support global communications and entrepreneurial studies to support business startups and professional development of international workforce populations. A lot has been done with our team of 45 people. Our staff is a scalable on demand workforce that is crowdsourced. When I say we have a staff of 45 people, that means we have 45 positions that are managed through a scalable crowdsourced environment that is accessed on-demand.

I'm about to start my second five-year terms starting January 1, 2020 in this position, I'm a civilian ambassador representing the interests of the United States and serving as the face of the United States as it relates to business education and technology.

Our team started this venture in the year 2015. Our second term begins in the year 2020 and continues for another five years ending in the year 2025. The regions we support while representing the United States is Asia, the middle East, Russia, the Commonwealth of independent States and South America. In all of these areas, we support business consulting for startups and entrepreneurs, providing education resources and technology support.

Specifically, as it relates to technology support, what we had done in our first term as a United States ambassadorship team is work with a company in Australia in the area of data collection that would later be used for machine learning, which in turn would support artificial intelligence. It is this artificial intelligence that would be used for virtual reality, augmented reality and augmented virtual reality. These representations would also be used not only for video or visual effects, but also for sound recognition such as used in the Google and Amazon digital voice assistant devices.

The educational resources provided through our office, are in the area of supporting international institutions, academies and schools. We continue that today in all areas including the Middle East, Europe, South America, Russia and the Commonwealth independent States.

We support global communications and entrepreneurial studies to support business startups and professional development of international workforce populations such as airline pilots that travel globally and international business leaders. A lot has been done with our team of 45 people. Our staff is a scalable on demand workforce that is crowdsourced. When I say we have a staff of 45 people, that means we have 45 positions that are managed through a scalable crowdsourced environment that is accessed on-demand.   It is an advanced modern approach to staffing. A lot of our methodology does not rely on older traditional methodologies.

As individuals staff members can come in and out and take on certain tasks. Our responsibility is to keep those positions active and open so that it is worthwhile for our staff to take part in a crowdsourced, scalable, on-demand workforce environment. We find this business model that supports international staffing to be most cost effective and can be sustained long-term.

If we were to think of the position of an ambassador, it could not be thought of in the same way as a regular job because it is not a job. It is a responsibility. It is a responsibility to maintain those 45 positions so that the office of the ambassadorship can continue and be sustained long term.

My role as an ambassador is not a job. It is a responsibility with significant sacrifice, but even greater rewards. (It's not for everyone) Moreover, it is not a job. It is an office that is managed. A simple way to understand this concept is I do not focus on my personal income and employment as this does not relate to what I do as an ambassador. Instead what I focus on is the livelihood of those 45 positions so it can be sustained long-term because without my team I could not be an ambassador. It is not possible. That being said, a civilian ambassador to the nations is not the kind of job you find in a newspaper or an online job posting. It is something that you are called to do by the nations.   Using modern technology, we have focused on a staffing methodology that uses a crowdsourced utilization of a scalable on demand workforce.

With the 45 people that we have, we have four primary departments. One is technology to support the internet connection at the destination from my home country. The second one is operations for scheduling in different time zones. The third one relates to client relations because without clients we don't have a base of operations. The final one relates to audit and compliance so that we operate in a legal fashion overseas and abroad as an ambassador to the nations. Our team's primary product is the export of services. We are very much involved with exports to other nations. In our case it is the export of services in some small way. It is also done by way of product. In terms of our books and our movies and TV shows and radio shows. In all cases we put value on it so that people pay for a product or service. Knowing that it has value. We have met a lot of interesting people during our journey. I work with children and adults directly. The process we use is called augmented virtual reality jumping because we are going through the firewalls of China and the developing firewall of Russia as well as others. Moreover, we are also touching each other by sharing a screen and able to see each other face to face.   That creates a true personal environment.

One of the beautiful things that we get to experience is to visit cultures in a way that tourists are not able to do. We are able to experience that desires and needs of civilians in other countries. You don't see that as a tourist because of the technology involved using augmented virtual reality and other tools such as web conferencing and more. I have been on a bus in Russia and in a taxi in Taiwan and on the street in China. I have been everywhere. I have walked upstairs with people. I've been in a coffee shop. I am working with people directly in their personal lives. People have shown me their pets. I have seen newborn babies. All that allows me to see more of the family and families that grow.

The connections that I make as a United States ambassador is very personal and that is the greatest reward going beyond all sacrifice. This makes it more important for me to represent the United States in a positive and productive way. We do this through encouragement and motivation and teaching. I have become very connected with many people. Citizens of other countries have shared recipes with me as well as me sharing recipes with them that support my passion and hobby of cooking that goes along with theirs. We bond in closeness with something in common. The cooking habits and working in a kitchen is one such example.

I bond with business leaders of all sizes as I have the ability to do that. Being a business leader myself since 1994 whatever experiences a new business startup is having, be it good or small. I've seen all of it and I guide business leaders through encouragement and motivation and education.

I have a passion of teaching and earned a master's degree in education in the year 1988. I enjoy developing the future of our world through teaching. That is one such example of being a United States ambassador to the nations by serving as faculty in international academies and institutions. Teaching is an extension of the business consulting that our office supports.

I am proud of the work that we have done for so many years. In addition to teaching, our team is very much involved with curriculum development, which guides the instruction and development of our teachers. Moreover, I recall serving as the Dean of teachers at one Academy that allowed me to directly influence the positive outcome of other teachers. All this experience comes from the foundation of being a professor at universities and colleges in the United States. My teaching experience to businesses directly come from the corporate training that I had conducted in the years that followed my earning of my master's degree in education in 1988 all previous experiences serve as a foundation of present-day activities.

People are a collection of their experiences and those experiences create knowledge which in turn is used as wisdom for decisions. At this point I have worked with so many nations and therefore so many cultures that when I make a decision, it is not a guess. It is a genuine fact. In terms of the right thing to do based on already knowing what the wrong thing to do is. My office of the ambassador ship is based on what we have called the models of excellence, the model of excellence serve as our core values, our core values focus on how we operate globally in Australia, Asia, the Middle East, Russia, Europe, and South America. These are the territories that we put great attention on.

Whatever we do, it effects our representation of the United States to these foreign nations. Our office is the face of America and people are watching us closely. We have the burden of responsibility to show America in a positive light that effect future economic outcomes and international relationships. It is in the best interest of the office of the ambassador to represent the United States in a positive light while performing good action in the areas of business consulting, providing educational resources and technology review and support. The big umbrella that covers what we do for business education and technology is global communication and entrepreneurial studies. Let me tell you what the models of excellence are.

The models of excellence is what we think about while performing our duties as it relates to our core values. The first one is motivation. The second one is organization. The third one is discipline. The fourth one is ethics. The fifth one is learning all the time. The last one is strength not to give up. These are the models of excellence. When we motivate people, our intention is to know that they have a future. When we help people become organized, it allows them to know what their future is. When we help people with their self-discipline, they are able to stay focused and on the path of their future. When we help people with their ethical awareness, we are having fully aware of the difference between right and wrong. When we help people with their learning and development, we are helping them to understand that learning is a lifelong process and it is a natural and necessary process as part of living and business. When we help people with strength, we're giving them the endurance to not give up on their future and so that is what our core values is all about. Again, our models of excellence serving as our core values relate to motivation, organization, discipline, ethics, learning and strength. Our team keeps thinking of this while we support global communication and entrepreneurial studies in the areas of business, education and technology.

As we plow through the nations helping to create a better world through our core values, we know that there are challenges and obstacles that we must avoid. Most of those challenges and obstacles come from other people. Very often myself as well as my staff receive derogatory comments and gossip. When you receive derogatory carbons or behavior from other people, it comes from one or more of three things. It boils down to three reasons. Those reasons are number one, a person can be intimidated by you. Number two, a person can be afraid of you. Number three, a person can be jealous of you. Let me say that again. Number one, a person can be intimidated by you. Number two, they can be jealous of you. Number three, they can be afraid of you. Those are the three primary reasons why someone would shoot a derogatory comment or behavior your way with no provocation. If you are aware that a person's odd behavior comes through their own intimidation of you or being afraid of you or being jealous of you, then you know that it's an obstacle that you can overcome because you understand what the sources. There are three ways to discern this type of behavior. Let's explore those three ways that these people might behave in a way toward you without provocation. That is derogatory in nature. The three-ways are deception, manipulation, and selfishness.

If people are derogatory towards you without provocation, you can discern it with the behaviors of deception, manipulation, or selfishness. Look at the behavior and you will see it will fall into one of those three categories. My office of the ambassador is protected with knowledge that produces wisdom. Knowing that derogatory action and derogatory behavior comes from either being jealous by another person, intimidated by another person, or afraid by another person. The opponent, if I could use that word, is jealous of you or afraid of you or intimidated by you. That's their problem. It's not your problem, especially if there's no provocation. The red flags that allow us to recognize these types of behaviors is the deceptive words or behavior that you pick up and the decisions the opponent makes that have conversation where it's obvious they're trying to manipulate you and the deception and manipulation comes from selfish behavior.

People who deceive and manipulate through selfish behavior are not your friends. They will not support you. They will support themselves. They need you more than you need them, but will not show it. If you can recognize this behavior, then you know who to avoid and not be engaged in the people you want to work with or associate yourself with are those who do not deceive and manipulate through selfish behavior. Moreover, there is no reason to entertain the connection with others who are either jealous of you or intimidated by you or afraid of you. It's not your problem and you'd need not spend any time on that foolishness. It is worthy of knowing that you can pick and choose the people that you are with. This includes family members. Some family members may need to be removed from your life and you have control to choose how that is done.

If you do not remove such people that we're talking about here, then they become a yoke of burden that holds you in captivity that can destroy you. You can be robbed of your success. If you allow that to happen, if you allow that to happen, the only person you can blame is yourself because you made the choice to enable that behavior to be bestowed upon yourself. Do not allow that to happen. As I say this, I'm not saying that it's easy. I know it is not. I know it because I have experienced it because I have removed the obstacles in my life. I am now able to be a successful ambassador to the nations in the civilian sector, in the areas of business, education and technology. It allows me to focus on our core values, which are the models of excellence. This is all that I wanted to talk about today.

Our office of the ambassadorship to the nations remembers our core values and purpose. Again, whatever we do, it effects our representation of the United States to these foreign nations. Our office is the face of America and people are watching us closely. We have the burden of responsibility to show America in a positive light that effect future economic outcomes and international relationships.

 My purpose of this discussion is to give you an understanding of what being an ambassador to the nations is all about. It is not a job. It is a responsibility of a team of people and managing those team of people through a set of core values represented by what we call the models of excellence in the areas of business, education and technology.

With this, there is a sacrifice. Good things come with a sacrifice for people of faith. They understand when they read the Bible that overcoming obstacles and successes and victories all come with sacrifice. It is a biblical principle. I am a man of God and I know this. It is wonderful to be an ambassador to the nations in multiple countries and continents. It has its rewards and benefits. At the same time. This role and responsibility come with significant sacrifice. One such example of a sacrifice is I work seven days per week. I do not complain. I love what I do. I would not make any changes. The rewards and benefits outweigh the negative attributes of the position (for lack of a better term).

My positions offers so many rewards that outweigh the sacrifices. I can see things and experience things in other nations that are not possible by a tourist who goes to those nations. This gives me more knowledge about other nations than people who have actually been there. A tourist might see great architecture and tastes great food. As an ambassador, I see the people and I see inside their hearts. You can't do that as a tourist. As an ambassador, I can affect the future of lives, which in turn affects to some small degree, the future of that nation. You can't do that as a tourist. It is a wonderful experience.

As we live our lives, each one of us hopes to leave behind some sort of legacy. Ambassadors can do that even in the civilian sector. It's a sacrifice, but well worth the price of that sacrifice.

As I look back in my life and think about the future, I consider what legacy I want to leave behind. Whatever that legacy is, history will determine how it is defined, but however history records it, I do want it to be globally impactful. It is interesting to note that when I started my business in 1994 in the state of Massachusetts in the United States, it would be only four years later that I would launch a subsidiary of my company called the new England publishers association that would support six new England States. Within four years. I was beyond the boundaries of my state of Massachusetts. Later in the years of 2004 to 2015 I had a lecture tour in the seven States of New York and New England reaching 52 venues. During 11 years, I covered the Northeast of the United States and did not focus on my local city or my home state. I gained an early experience going beyond the boundaries. In the year 2015 I formally went beyond the boundaries of my home country. It was

December of 2013 that I went beyond the boundaries of my home country in an informal way, but shortly thereafter that's when I became an ambassador to the nations in the civilian sector specializing in entrepreneurial business, education service, and technology support.

My conversation today is not to have a parade or blow a horn that is self-serving. I do not speak to you in a prideful way. I am not presenting this to pat myself on my back. I'm sharing with you a journey that I have. It is not a common journey. It is a journey of sacrifice with significant rewards.

Some people who take on this role in challenge do not succeed very often. They do not finish their first five year term. I am honored to have been able to launch my second five year terms starting in the year 2020 to be able to start a second five year term means that the first five year term was completed successfully. The reason why the second five year term could be launched was because of three things that relate to our three areas of responsibility, which are business, education and technology.

In the summer before the start of my second five-year term, my company celebrated 25 years in business. That is a quarter of a century in the year prior to that, 12 books were published representing each month of the year and we're called the silver anniversary series. In preparation for the 25 year anniversary, which occurred in July of 2019. in August of 2019, which was before the start of the second five-year term, I had been awarded two international certificates in education, which required a large sacrifice of time. The last qualification has a little bit of a longer story. I will make the story short here. At Harvard university in the year 1951 my father discovered hydrogen in space during Easter weekend. It relates to a field of science called radio astronomy. During the summer of 2019 I had reached out to the astrophysics department at Harvard university to consider a 70th anniversary of the discovery of hydrogen in space that would be recognized or observed in the year 2021. In my email that I sent, it included a six minute video that came from a TV show that showed my father and his doctoral thesis advisor discussing what happened in 1951 when hydrogen was discovered in space. Eight minutes after I sent the email, I got a response. If you think about how long an email is sent and then read and then viewing a six-minute video, then you can understand that a response with an eight minutes is basically instantaneous. It was as if it was pre-destined and meant to be.

There was an agreement that we would start working on this celebration or observance sometime in the spring, in the year of 2020 so that the celebration could occur in the year 2021 this in itself was about 33% of the reason why my second five year term was authorized because I satisfied the requirement of technology in addition to the business in education that had previously been done. Our earlier technology work had previously been done with a data gathering in Australia. Now we're working with Harvard University with the celebration of a significant scientific discovery done in 1951.

All of the three things that associated with the accomplishment of goals and recognition in terms of business education in technology happened during the summer of 2019 for business. It was 25 years in business for education. It was the two international certifications for technology. It was the affiliation and the work being planned and approved. Uh, in August of 2019 all of these three things were not planned, and it was not known that they would coincide at the same time in terms of a pinnacle success. These are the reasons why my second five-year term was authorized.

The only thing that was necessary was my approval. I signed off and approved that our office and team of 45 staff members would move forward for the next five years. As the office of ambassadorship continues in its second five-year voyage, we will have the benefit of new technology that is internet related and mobile network related allowing us to have an even greater augmented virtual reality experience that was not possible before. That being said, our impact in our second five-year term will even be greater than our first five-year term. That is why I signed off and approved that the office of the ambassadorship in the civilian sector for business education and technology be continued because it would serve a greater purpose with even greater victories.

That being said, our calling to serve as ambassador to the nations in the civilian sector was absolutely necessary and could not be avoided. We have a much greater purpose because we'll have a greater impact as we have done before. We have affected the future of people's lives. We've given them encouragement. We've given them motivation. We've given them hope. These things that we give are done through love. This is also a biblical principle. That is what we're supposed to do with our fellow man. However, we are doing it through the office of the ambassadorship and doing it globally. It is something that I could not refuse.

I close out my conversation as I feel at this point you may have a better understanding of what it means to be an ambassador to the nations. It is a position of sacrifice. It is a position of necessity. It is not a position of nobility and respect living in a palace and riding around in limousines. There are huge sacrifices, but the benefits outweigh the sacrifices.

I believe I will continue as an ambassador for the rest of my life, working very hard as I'm physically able to impact the needs of the nations in the area of business, education and technology through our core values represented by motivation, organization, discipline, ethics, learning and strength.

I am guided by the teachings of the Bible. Our Lord and savior gives me the strength to do what I do, and I thank the Lord for showing me the light to continue on this journey for as long as I'm physically able.

I thank you for attending and being attentive to my conversation today. I bless you all. Thank you, and good day.